CW00859328

Dreaming in a Perfect World

Dreaming in a Perfect World

Amazon Self-Publishing
Kindle Direct Publishing

Dreaming in a Perfect World

Other Works by The Author

<u>Fiction</u>

God is a Woman
Far From Heaven

<u>Poetry</u>

Don't Wait Til I Die To Love Me
Nirvana: Pieces of Self-Healing vol. 1
& 2
Young Heart, Old Soul
Songs for Each Mood
A Day Without Sun

<u>**Collabs w/ Moonsoulchild**</u>

Self Talks
Heal, Inspire, Love

To the reader:

As you read the contents of this book
please be mindful of a few things, 1)
dreams can get really weird 2) a lot of
the dreams were handwritten in the dark
or rushed as I have naturally lousy
handwriting, so I apologize for any
errors you may see in the dreams
scanned into this book. I wanted to
give you all the rawest versions of
each dream I decided not to rewrite or
type them. Grammar police relax lol. I
hope you all enjoy the dreams I
featured, as it took a lot of courage
to show this side of me. I hope you all
enjoy the poems even more.

Another Note for the reader:

Our dreams contain so many messages we often overlook. They express our deepest fears, passions, and most suppressed memories. I hope this book inspires you to pay more attention to your dreams. Each poem is an interpretation of each dream, so may hit home to you, some may not make any sense at all, but every poem is pure in its rawest form. With that said, I must forewarn themes of sexual abuse, violence, sexual concepts, and mental illness that may not be suited for minors or people who struggle with these issues are contained in this book. As you continue to read I hope my words help you cope with your struggles, I hope these words can help you grow. Above all, I want you to know you are not alone

Dreaming in a Perfect World

Dream #2: Strength

I was totally ill and crippled. Every breath
was I labored for every breath,
My pride refused any help offered
I was too stubborn to accept my
fate. I continued to walk on my own.
Even through my disability I had hope.
I was relentless. I had the power, the will
to move on my own, even when the
task felt impossible

Dreaming in a Perfect World

<u>After 'Dying to Live' by Edgar Winter</u>

Somedays the sun
begs me to wake up
when my body feels anchored
to the bed,
because the outside world
seems too grim
to explore.

Sometimes the warmth
From my blanket
Feels like a shield
From this cold world,
when staying in bed seems like
The resolution to my problems

I try to convince myself
it's better to live in fear
than to go outside,
There's no use in living
If I'm just living to die

The sun grows more relentless
in its pursuit
to get me out into the world.

Eventually, I concede,
brush my teeth,
Eat breakfast,
Get dressed,
And start my day.
I thank the sun
and its clouds
For not giving up on me.

Dreaming in a Perfect World

Just because the world
is filled with sadness
and void of compassion
it doesn't mean
I gotta follow suit.
I wasn't born to fit in.

The Doctor

Time is the greatest doctor
When you give him the patience
to heal you.
As he devotes every minute
Of daylight to help
Sow each wound
And mend your fragmented heart.
All he asks of you
Is to trust the process
There's so much to learn
When you take your time

Lessons my Father Taught Me

I was 5
Running as fast as the wind
could chase me
My clumsy foot
tripped and stumbled
over a crack
On the sidewalk,
A slight burning sensation
I felt on my knee
Followed by blood
Running to my ankle
I cried because
Pain was a foreign concept
Impossible to understand,
My father ran to me and said
"you'll be alright."
A few days later
I was picking at the scab
covering my wound,
My father said
"Stop touching, so it can heal."
When I listened,
A scar formed a few days later
But tougher skin appeared,
Over time I learned
About falling and getting up
Healing pains and after scars,
My father taught me one lesson
no matter how bad it hurts
Never pick at your wounds
Give them time to heal

Love in the Sun

I hope your days
Begin to glow brighter
I hope you wake up
Knowing every breath
You take is golden
You are worth
Every ounce of love
The sun shines
Upon you

Sad Bird

Even with broken wings
The sad bird still sings
Despite being unable to take flight
The sad bird still sings at night

Black women Deserve Rest Too

Black women deserve a break from
wearing the iron suit. When are they
allowed to be soft and vulnerable? They
fight every day to protect the people
they love, but who shows up for them
when they feel outnumbered? We praise
black women for being strong yet
neglect they need protection too. Their
shoulders often carry more tension than
bricks after a long day of carrying
their burdens. Sometimes they wanna
take off their cool. Be free,
unguarded. Black women deserve rest
too. I've peered into the restless eyes
of my mother, aunts, sisters, cousins,
friends, strangers and knew their
'tired' was different from mine. They
shouldn't have to put up a wall to be
respected. They shouldn't have to go
through hell to be loved. They deserve
to be soft without feeling guilty.

Sometimes I Wonder if God hates black people

O God,
What did we do to deserve
such suffering with no mercy?
Are we the bastard children
You claim with shame?
Why must
Our prayers go neglected
As we traverse under the sun
Without your protection?
Please answer my question,
We fight to climb
The rope of hope
But it's brittle and soaked
You've made it impossible
To hold on,
You watched my ancestors
get whipped until
The skin on their backs
Resembled bark on trees
You witnessed black people
get hung until their blood
Showered the leaves
Like the rain
you pour down
On us relentlessly,
Where were you
As houses were burned
And churches were bombed
As they sang hymns and songs
In your honor
Why do you turn a blind eye

Dreaming in a Perfect World

Every time we're hunted
By beasts,
Like antelope in the wild?
How does your heart
not feel sorrow
When a melanated child
Is robbed of tomorrow?
You claim to love all
of your creations
Yet somehow
It seems like you deserted
Us in this cold,
Without your warmth
And hated by a nation

"Try to understand a person's trauma
and fears before calling them crazy,
it's shallow and dismissive. When you
refuse to dig deep enough to love them,
your surface-level thinking becomes
part of the problem."

Dream 3 # Wet Dreams

It's 2am, in my Mixtee's guest room.
The scent of french toast & bacon settled
in the air. Sam woke up as I yawned.

"Oh good morning," She said
as my love pistol poked your back.
I attempted to get out of bed, but you
pushed me down.
"What are you doing?" I whispered
You seduced me with your stare, and
bit your lower Lip.
My hands began to caress your body
"eat me" you said softly.
"We might not have time" I responded

I massaged your clit until wetness arrived
You mounted me, I palmed your mouth
the door was cracked open. we couldn't
afford to be loud.

Permission

Allow my hands to dance
on your electric body
giving them the freedom
to enjoy the party of a lifetime,
sparks fly when they touch you.

Let these hands
Travel to that divine island
Until wetness surround
Your inner thighs
I'll back stroke
Inside your ocean
'til the waves subside.

Baby, my love pistol
is loaded
I'm ready to pull
the trigger on you

I just need your permission
To give your body
The kind of passion
That'll leave your eyes rolling
Into next week.

Role Play

Tonight,
let's escape to a new world
In this bed of ours,
become who you want
And I will play my part,
New found strangers in the dark
As our hearts spark
Like lightening,
shockwaves flow through
Our bodies,
In this theater we made
our bedroom is the stage
Everything is a prop
During role play,
Be whoever you wanna be
As long as you match my energy
Loving inside you, naturally
Never feels the same
When you introduce
me to a new you, intimately

The Art of Making Love II

no need to rush
When making love
Your body is a canvass
As I stroke with my brush, girl
Painting hues onto
The shape of you
To rhythm and blues,
Love in your eyes
We create art after midnight
A masterpiece
between the sheets
When we arrive

Dream - Moving On

My friends and I were walking into
a house party. Then I saw Her,
the woman who broke my heart twice.

She reached for me, but I kept walking.
She screamed my name, I ignored.
It felt good to be free from her grips.

As I walked into the party, I danced
and smiled and got happily drunk, As
She stood outside alone.

"Outgrowing people you grew up with is
a different kind of heartbreak, but
it's necessary."

Why We Didn't Work?

Emotions tossed out into the snow
Because your ego grew too cold
Now we've grown apart,

Your pride spoke louder
than the truth
And it clouded your
fragile ego,
We were broken long
before the goodbyes
Traveled to the tips
of our tongues

Now it's time
to leave it all behind,
Your stubbornness led us
to a dead end
And I gotta find my way
back home without you,
A reality that had
to come true
so, we could part ways
and take the road
we were meant to travel, alone.

Heartbreak City

I've traveled so far
that heartache has become
a foreign land
my GPS can't detect
I no longer speak
the same language
Or relate to the culture
To be honest,
I wouldn't recognize
that place
If I comeback today,
And I have no intentions
on visiting again,
I'm in love with where I'm at
And eager to see
my future ahead,
I refuse to waste mileage
Revisiting the place
that tried to break me,

Burning Home

The house we built no longer
feels like home,
it's time to set
the drapes on fire
And watch the walls burn
'til the memories we share
Turn to ashes and dust,
We must vacate this place
before our lungs
Inhale too much smoke
We gotta take different routes
To escape, my dear
There's no need to save
whatever good we have left
Let the blaze choose its fate
It's time for my heart
to build a new home
without you,
I hope you have the courage
to do the same

Hello 2morrow

Many of us are reluctant to say goodbye
to people, places, or things because we
fear the unknown of a new tomorrow. I
say, bury that fear; overtime, you'll
gradually witness a new you emerging
from the soil. You only get one chance
to live in your present body, don't
waste it on holding the past hostage.
Tomorrow is eager to meet you, don't
disappoint it by trying to water dead
roots.

Trying to Forget

I'm trying to forget the pain, but the
scars on my broken heart remind me of
the past.

Time

Time is of the essence
Don't waste it on giving
someone fifteen 2nd chances.

Tug of War

You should never play tug of war with
your peace. Some people only come into
your life to disrupt your bliss. Your
peace is not a game and when someone
decides to tug and pull, let go of the
rope and watch them fall as your peace
remains intact.

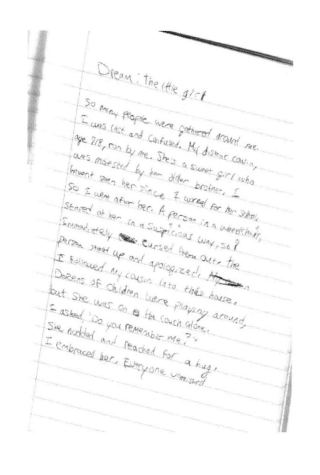

Dream: The little girl

So many people were gathered around me.
I was lost and confused. My distant cousin,
age 7/8, ran by me. She's a sweet girl who
was molested by her older brother. I
havent seen her since I cared for her school.
So I went after her. A person in a wheelchair
stared at her in a suspicious way, so I
Immediately cursed them out. The
person stood up and apologized.
Dozens of children were playing around,
but she was on the couch alone.
I asked, "Do you remember me?"
She nodded and reached for a hug.
I embraced her. Everyone vanished.

To the Little Girl with the Shy Smile and Sad Eyes

When those disturbing words
traveled to my ears,
the reality pinched
until my skin
was covered in bruises,
My stomach twisted into knots
I couldn't untie
the disgust for 5 days,
My tears formed a river for
the pain you suffered
At the hands of your brother,
my cousin,
someone I grew up with,
My mind swirled
into thoughts of disbelief,
I couldn't fathom,
him being capable
Of stealing
his sister's innocence

I wanted to clamp my hands
around his neck
Until air was incapable
of passing through
His lungs
I wanted to watch him
Beg for his life.

Unfortunately,
by the time I heard the news
he was already
a thousand miles away
In the army,

Dreaming in a Perfect World

Living the second chance
he didn't deserve
And you were left confused,
In a broken home

time had passed,
I was hired to work
at your school At first
I thought you'd reject me,
That seeing me
would remind you of him
But every morning you would wave
Tell me about your previous day
And gave a hug before

you walked to class,
We're not related by blood
but I saw you as my own, still do
I wish I could've
protected you from
that cold-blooded bastard

I hope you know,
It's wasn't your fault,
it never will be
As you grow older
And find ways to cope
with the purity
He tried to rob from you
I pray it never breaks you,
You're already stronger
than you'll ever know
His filthy hands

Dreaming in a Perfect World

may have touched
your surface
but they didn't
penetrate your soul

Please continue to smile,
find reasons to laugh
always go outside and play
never grow cold and numb
allow your heart to feel
as you learn how to heal

Fighting

She is fighting to be understood by
people who counted her out. Climbing
from the bottom to get noticed by
people who don't care. I hope, by the
time she reaches the top; she will no
longer feel the need to be validated
by irrelevant people.

Who Will Cry

Who will cry for the child
That wears a smile to hide despair
Who will cry for the child
When no one seems to care

Who will cry for the child
Forced to grow up too fast
Who will cry for the child
Forever running from their past

Who will cry for the child
slowly losing wonder and hope
Who will cry for the child
Whose been hurt by someone close

Who will cry for the child
That wallows in self-shame
Who will cry for the child
That bares all the blame

Who will cry for the child
Dealing with wounds
covered in salt
Who will cry for the child
Healing from scars
they didn't cause

Who will cry for the child
That was taught abuse is affection
Who will cry for the child
growing up without protection

I will cry for the child,
The child feeling lost at home
I will cry for the child
To let them know,
They are not alone

Consent II

There are too many classes teaching
daughters how to defend themselves
Against predators, but no classes
teaching sons how to respect the space
of women. The concept of consent is
foreign to so many men, and I wonder
where did the parents go wrong? Why do
so many men feel entitled to bodies
that don't belong to them? Why do they
feel the need to pressure women to get
what they want? Why do they feel so
comfortable with invading their
personal space? Why does society
enable this behavior? Why do men lack
the empathy to understand?

My Uncle, The Predator

My father's oldest brother
Was a Predator
And it wasn't a secret
More like a running joke
He wasn't the
"flirt with younger girls" type
He was the
"break into a woman's house, in the
nude, and hold her at knife point" type
He would get caught,
Go to jail for a few months,
Come out,
Repeat cycle,
He said he enjoyed jail;
The small room,
Crappy food,
The chaos,
The solitude,
My family often
made jokes about his horrid acts
I laughed along
Because that's what we do
as black families
Turn tragedy into comedy
My uncle,
Got caught
Jerking off outside
A woman's window
During his last run
He went to jail, 90 days

Dreaming in a Perfect World

Got out
Then got sent back to Arkansas
We haven't heard from him
in 15 years,
I also have cousins and uncles
who went to jail
on petty drug charges,
Served time of 3,5,10 years
I'm not saying
it's okay to sell dope
But for them to do more time,
Than a serial sex predator
Shows how the judicial system
Couldn't care less about
the safety of women
and children

I feared the old perv more than the drug dealers

The drug dealers protected me,
The drug dealers gave me money
For store runs
The drug dealers gave me
fly hand me downs
and put me on game
I was always sad
when the drug dealers
Went away for
extended vacations,
but when they came back
they always
Complimented my height
and asked about football,
The drug dealers never posed
any harm to me
They loved me, for real
unlike the old man
With the old van,
And lived in the old house
all alone
He offered candy
when it wasn't Halloween,
He was extra nice
to little boys like me
we were never allowed
to walk past his house alone.
He would say hey
We would ignore
We heard the stories
of him exposing himself 'for fun.'
The old man creeped us out,
His yellow eyes and teeth
Were far from welcoming,

Dreaming in a Perfect World

I was always disappointed
Because he never left
for extended vacations
Like the drug dealers did

Drunken Jokes Behind Sober Pain

On many nights
Under the starry sky
With my dad, uncle, and aunt
I vividly remember
The wild stories they told
From their youth,
In Shady Grove, Arkansas
Over beers and cheap vodka
Like sightings of
talking cats, UFOs,
Dogs and Ghosts
It was hard to believe
These drunken folklores
Because the stories
Seemed like
Delusions from extreme
heat and boredom
But the stories they told about
Their estranged brother
stuck out the most
My father would say,
"He would slap his dick across
Our face, when we were sleeping."
My uncle would laugh,
And say *"he called it a 'free gift,'*
then punched us when we cried"
Their drunken laughs
Would echo through
the silent night air.

Dreaming in a Perfect World

I laughed along,
Thinking it was hilarious
Because I was a child
Bottle after bottle
Cup After Cup
They would drink until
The cooler of ice
Melted into dirty warm Water
It wasn't until I grew
into my adulthood I realized
They used drunk jokes to
Soothe their sober pain
'Cause their innocence
was shattered like broken glass,
And alcohol
is cheaper than therapy

Dream: High School

I was walking the halls of my high school,
not as a teen, but as my ~~past~~ current self.
Students greeted me with hugs and
high-fives. I wasnt perceived as ~~a~~
socially awkward, weird, or a loser.
~~I was~~ I was seen as the cool kid,
~~the~~ ~~a~~ complete opposite of what I experienced
during my H.S years. Girls wanted me,
the guys wanted to be around me, I was
excelling in sports and academics.

But why am I an adult in H.S., I asked
myself. Everyone seems unbothered or
unaware by this. Do they see me as
an adult, or one of them?

If I could have a conversation with my 17 year old self here's what I would say

Stand up for yourself,
Until you're the tallest
in the room
Rise up my friend
so no one can belittle you

speak with your chest,
Let the clouds hear you
Loud and proud
So when rain falls
It will wash away your doubts

Don't carry those burdens
Your shoulders
don't deserve the strain
The only way to heal
Is by confronting the pain
Face to face,

The world is cold,
It's not your fault
You possess an old soul
And a warm heart

If I could have a conversation with my 17-year-old self, here's what I would say II

I. It's okay to move at your own pace, wear the clothes that make you feel good, never chase trends, and listen to the music you want to hear. You were not born to follow trends or fit in. People only bully you because 1) they're insecure in their own skin, 2) they were too closed-minded to understand you.

II. Popularity is fleeting and means nothing in the real world. You can't put your high school social status on your resume'. And what if I told you that most of the 'cool' kids peaked in high school. That's right some of them are more lost now than ever, because they were hollow on the inside. Once they got into the real world, they had nothing to offer

Take this time to focus inward. that's where your true beauty and Value is, my friend.

III. You found your purpose in life and living it. The High school experience will become a major part into who you will eventually. So stay strong, don't crack. It's almost over, you will be free from this hell they called school

Dreaming in a Perfect World

When my Anxiety was Born

Walking the halls
of high school,
Made me feel like the ceiling
would fall at any moment,
And the floor was covered
in egg shells
As I had to
tiptoe my way to class

Very few people
respected my space
As they smacked
the back of my neck and ran
And everyone spit
on my feelings
When they called me
'can't get right'

It was embarrassing to
be known as
the biggest screwup
on the football field
by the entire student body

Students and teachers
Who barely knew my name
Would yell 'can't get right'
when I walked by.
I would laugh with
a smile on my face
But in my mind
I envied turtles
Because they have
the ability
to hide in a shell,
But I had to face

Dreaming in a Perfect World

this reality
185 days for four years.

I was the skinny
soft-spoken kid
With the mustache
not fully grown in
So they called me 'Hitler'

I was too weird
for the black kids
Not emo enough for the whites
I wore oversized-overpriced
clothes to fit in,
But all the jocks
would grab my shirt
To check the tag,
"This shit fake'
they would say
Everyone believed them,
Without listening to me

Everyone was obsessed
with sex,
I was okay with
moving at my pace
I got mocked
for being a virgin,
Even girls cracked jokes

I was the school's
verbal punching bag
Every day was a battle,
Until I stopped fighting,

Dreaming in a Perfect World

I realized bullies
Used me to project their
insecurities Onto me.

I became content with being
misunderstood
I began to fall in love
with who I was becoming

Even though high school sucked
It built some character
If I could,
I wouldn't change a thing.

But I'm not Homophobic

In high school,
I used to say things like
"I don't care
if you're gay as long as you
Don't come around me with it"
As if gay was a drug my peers
were getting high off,
I would say
"That's so gay"
Or let my tongue
Launch Fag bombs
Into the air
And watched them explode
as lighthearted insults
To my friends
But "I'm not homophobic"
I would say
When a gay kid got picked
on or beat up
I said nothing,
I did even less,
I was even casted
in a school play
But declined the role
Because the character was gay
But swore I wasn't homophobic
"I tolerate them"
I would say

Dreaming in a Perfect World

A few years later
I was in college
A rising artist
Was my new obsession
I wanted to dress like him,
Sing like him,
He inspired me
to become a writer
As I wrote
Verses and poems
Just like he would.
His name: Frank Ocean
One night, he came out
Professed to the world
about his love affair
with a man
"How could I connect
with a man who's gay"
I said,
my perception was shattered
Because I realized
I was in fact homophobic
The thought of idolizing
a bi-sexual man
was something I couldn't fathom,
His lyric
"I believe that marriage isn't
Between a man
and woman but between love and love"
Took on a new meaning,
I didn't hear before.
Slowly,
my ice cold homophobia
Began to melt

Dreaming in a Perfect World

Into a puddle of regret,
I felt the guilt rushing
through my bones.

My ignorant ears
Were finally willing to listen
Thanks to Frank Ocean
My mental state, ascended
I learned that love must
be supported unconditionally
or not at all.

I transitioned
from ignorant to understanding
Thank God for Frank Ocean,
He helped me see
What's right

Dream : Social Distancing

My Father, sisters, and I were
shopping for groceries. The store was
empty. No supplies or customers.
The only items left were a stack of
video games. A demo called "end of days 0"
was presented on the big screen. It was
horrific. Deady robots and transformers
destroying earth.
"Can I buy this." I asked
"Were closing." an associate says
"but can I get it."
I find my family and urged them to
leave. My intuition knew something
was going to happen. My father pulled
out of his parking spot. A woman
nearly rearended him.

"Should we tell her they're closed?"
I asked,
"Hell no." My dad said.

The Covid World

We treat each other like
walking viruses
Can't tell if
we're straight-faced
or smiling
Behind these fabric masks,
Tip toeing down the aisles
When they walk past,
Performing gymnastics
to get around my shopping cart,
Staying 6 feet apart,
at all cost
People act like they would melt
If I came any nearer
This feels like a shitty
Episode of black mirror
The death stares
when I cough or sneeze,
Like what the fuck
It's allergy season,
I loathe going outside
these days
I'm over life being
this way

Stream of Consciousness I

Mother Earth spins faster
Than usual
As if she's in a rush
for us to die soon
I don't blame her
Each day seems
to blend in with the last
Friday feel like Wednesday
5pm feels like 10am,
Nothing makes sense,
This place is a shitshow at best
tragedy is normal here
We've become immune to bad news
I wish I could get abducted
Along with everyone I love
by aliens
Start over in a new galaxy
Mother Nature
is spinning too fast
The grays in my hair
Remind me of that

We Need Love Now More Than Ever

Love is the answer
to all of our fears and anxiety,
sadly, affection
may cause an infection
upon those we love the most,

Standing six feet away
may save a loved one from
being thrown into
a six-foot dirt hole

Which is difficult
when I need a hug,
or when I see a friend
on the brink of a meltdown
love is needed
now more than ever,
unfortunately,
spreading that
can be deadly too

Dream: Running

I was running down a long endless
road. I was alone. I kept looking
back to see if I was being chased
by someone or something, but nothing
was there. The more I ran the
long the road stretched. Street lights
shined down on me. My body became
numb from the winter air, but I kept
running

Forrest Gump may Understand

Running far, far away
Until my feet get fatigued,
And legs beg me to stop
feels like the best way
To elude my woes
Then those demons
catch up to me
And ask
'are you ready to stop running?"
 a question I never have
the answer to
So I keep
running into a dead end
after dead end

Will I ever muster
the courage to stop running?
I may never know
But I do know,
My stamina would
Make Forrest Gump proud

What I learned from Cheetahs

Life flies by faster
than eyes blink,
never lose sight of the moment
When your mind tries to overthink

Stay calm under pressure
Life is not a race
Growth is not a competition
Heal at your own pace

Chase after your sunlight
Until happiness is in close sight
Never shorten your strides
Don't stop until life expires

Appreciate every yesterday
But never chase the past
Beautiful tomorrows wait ahead
keep runnin' fast,
Any moment could be your last

Dreaming in a Perfect World

A typical day as a 10-year-old boy in the Hood

The sound of fireworks
cracked the air
A few houses down,
But it wasn't the Fourth of July,
2am on a school night,
The noise startled me enough
to jump out of bed,
A series of heavy knocks
Shook the termites
That lived in the old wooden door
The bright light
Frightened the roaches
As they scurried
Across the kitchen floor
I tiptoed to see
What was going on
My cousin sobbed,
hysterically
with red paint
covering his palms
My pregnant mother said
"call the cops"
My father told me
to go back to sleep
But I couldn't move
My cousin,

Dreaming in a Perfect World

seemed to be in great pain
I needed to know why
he was playing with
paint and fireworks
Seemed like a fun time to me
Until a pistol fell
from his pocket
and he said
"I think she's dead"

Dream # The Storm

The night was filled with thunder and rain. Sara and I were sleeping, In a pitch black room. the bed was unfamiliar. A tree branch kept knocking on the window. the bedroom door cracked open, allowing a sliver of light in. I closed the door. It opened again, then I closed it. After a few more attempts, I gave up and went back to sleep. the wooden floor creaks. A dark figure enters the room. The temperature became hot. Sara remained asleep. The dark figured seemed to pose no harm as it stared at me. My heart raced, I couldn't rest.

Dark Thoughts

To the people who doubt themselves
into an anxiety attack
To the people who overthink
themselves into depression
It's easy to allow those dark
thoughts to consume you

Please, relax
Stop abusing yourself
You're not a failure

You're not falling behind
because things aren't happening
when you want them to
your dreams are miles ahead
Keep pacing
There's no need to rush

Dreaming in a Perfect World

Keep Swinging

My biggest fear is losing
her to my demons,
So I'll keep swinging
and punching
'til the fight is over
She's my motivation

Dreaming in a Perfect World

There Goes My Mind...again

I try to balance my thoughts
On a tightrope at 2am
Too bad I'm a clumsy gymnast

I create solutions
for problems that don't exist
And see the future
In a false reality
I'm a horrible psychic

I play tug of war with
My insecurities
While ignoring
All positive thoughts
Sometimes I lack the strength
To believe in myself

Why, does my mind
Play tricks on me?
I know I'm great
Or am I?
Fuck, I'm doing it again

Petals

Just like the rose that bloomed
after the storm, you too will
grow; despite being broken after
years of heartache and tears,
you too will flourish after the
dark clouds looming over your
reveal your silver lining.

Dreaming in a Perfect World

When The Sky Cries

Sometimes I sit outside
to watch the sky cry,
beautiful pain pours
From its silver-grey clouds,
Anger shakes the ground
When its thunderous voice
Screams loud enough
make the ground shake,
I love when the sky
Lets out such raw emotion
With unashamed openness,
On the days I feel hopeless
I can count on the sky
To make me feel less lonely
When the sky cries
the world listens intently
People slow down,
They go home.
Trees glisten
with beads of tears
Dripping off
the tip of their limbs
Some may fear
The thunder and lightening
I'm never frightened,
'Cause The sky is here to cry
When my eyes feel dry

Dreaming in a Perfect World

Dream: Lost Little Boy

I was a little boy in the ~~reality~~ Middle of nowhere.
The sun began to set and nature's sounds
echoed in the air. Crickets, ~~chirped~~ ~~is~~ ruffling
bushes. I was started all alone. I took off
in a sprint as fast as my legs could. Tears
flooded my eyes. I ~~dont~~ didnt know where
to go. I was a lost boy without a
helping hand

Boys 2 Men

As little boys,
we were taught to fight
our own battles,
never shed a tear,
and showing emotion
is a weakness,
The same little boys
who needed affection
when pain outweighed
their heavy heart,
Or compassion when
anxiety rattled their minds,
grew up to be men
with stone hearts
And closed minds
Because society only noticed
Their pain when they lashed
out with their fists
The same way people don't notice
a little boy's cry for help
Until he acts out in class
I urge you to
listen to the cries
that pour from the sad
little boy's eyes.
Boys need hugs too

90s baby woes

I regret
taking my childhood
for granted
I wish I could
negotiate a deal
with father time
so I could erase every
"can't wait 'til I grow up"
From my ungrateful tongue,
I miss the orange
VHS tape days,
The All That
and Good Burger days,
I miss running
from stray dogs
and kill
the carrier football,
Going inside just in time
To watch Goku's spirit bombs
and 106 & Park.
Playing Pokémon on my green
Gameboy color
Or scoring 40 points with Kobe
On Nintendo 64
I should've listened
to the adults
When they told me
to go slow

Dreaming in a Perfect World

And enjoy being a child
I was so eager to see the world
for what it is
now I miss being blissfully ignorant
living each day like a rugrat
I wish, I knew how good I had it

Dreaming in a Perfect World

"I often find myself missing the
childhood days I will never get back. I
wish there was a way I could feel those
moments again, to remind me how
precious time really is."

Dreaming in a Perfect World

Dream: In Love

Me and Moon were ~~invited~~ invited to vacay
on a yacht. We ~~got ready~~ accepted. The
water was crystal blue, the view from our
charter suite was gorgeous, the room was
decorated in white & gold. Gold bottles of
~~wine~~ champagne chilled on ice. The vibe
was right. No one bothered us as we
relaxed & ate good food. It was true
paradise.

Sober Karaoke

It's adorable how
she sings along to songs
she hardly knows
the lyrics to
Joyfully humming
and mumbling the melody until
she catches her favorite line,
The cute little dance she does
When the bridge arrives
Melts my heart into a puddle
Then she rolls her eyes
Over to my direction
To sing the chorus
From the bottom of her diaphragm
Off-key and tone-deaf
I smile,
cover my face and say
"You sound beautiful babe."
Her cheeks turn cherry
She playfully slaps my arm
"You're such a liar."
She laughs.
These little moments
are why true love
Is worth living for.

Dreaming in a Perfect World

A Song Like Poem

The sun smiles
every time you open your eyes,
why is he so eager
to greet you baby?
cause just like me
he loves to kiss the
the surface of your skin

Why does
the moon and her stars
gather at night?
'cuz when you dream
just like me
they long to hold you tight

When father time
and mother nature
decided to have a child
out of the sky blue
they made hair
from cloud dust
and created eyes
from crystal light
then came you.

Dreaming in a Perfect World

The angels got together
formed a bond so strong
and vowed to protect
you from harm
then brought us
to each other, baby
so we would create a love
to soft and warm

and that is why I
will never let you go
no
no
no
no
I will never let you go

Beautiful Addiction

Since the hands of yours
and mine first intertwined
Not A moment has gone by
That I don't feel loved
As the hands of time
slow dance around the clock
Each moment between you and I
Is filled with the type of love
Only the stars and moon
can relate to
Baby, you're the sun to my sky,
we bring each other light
so warm and bright
when the world becomes a storm,
We find solace under the rain
Our love is a home
I can't get enough of you
You're my beautiful addiction

No Goodbyes

I knew love
Lived in those eyes
The moment you smiled
And your lips said hi
since then
we never said goodbye

Dreaming in a Perfect World

Dream: The chase

I was shirtless and barefooted sprinting
through a foggy woods. Sweat covered
my body like baby oil. I was gassed.
The sound of shotguns blasting echoed in the air
as I ducked in the opposite direction.
I felt like a deer as I was being hunted
by a group of white men yelling
frantically, "Get that nigger!"
I knew death was my only outcome.

Hunting Season

"Justice for _____"
trends for the umpteenth time,
'cause another black life
becomes a new hashtag
as their soul
ascends to the sky

"Another one" I shake my head,
As I read about another
unarmed black person dead
In the headline once again
For reasons unexplained

I've seen this story so often
My heart is exhausted
From all the lives lost
My warm blood has frosted

I'm numb to the news
when we encounter a white hood
Or a suit that's blue
We know what they might do
See, as black people
We envy deer
They get a season
While we're hunted all year
We live
in a state of paranoia, fear

The hunters are always out
Looking for a new game
It's target practice everyday
And when you're black

Dreaming in a Perfect World

They have perfect aim

God gave us the speed
to dodge bullets,
but why not a bulletproof back?
that's where hunters
Shoot when they attack

just like deer
When we're hunted dead
Most of the world
Refuses to care
Because our lives
Is viewed as less valuable
In the eyes of many,

And just like deer
We hear many excuses
As to why we deserve
to die to justify
The hunter's actions

Dreaming in a Perfect World

Racism in America is like Middle School

Imagine being bullied
by the same group
of punks everyday
At first you refuse
to retaliate hoping
the hate fades away
But nothing changes,
After 2months
you try to make peace
You give them your shoes,
bike, and lunch money,
You beg and plea
For them to leave
Yet and still nothing changes,
You ask onlookers to help you
fight the bullies away,
They say
"that got nothing to do with me"
Or "I'm against violence"
Better yet, "Remain silent",
NOTHING FUCKING CHANGES
After a year
of being a target of hate
In what's should
be a safe space
You finally crack and break

Dreaming in a Perfect World

You defend yourself, Enraged
You grab
and throw anything you can,
Still nothing changes,
You feel you don't belong
The bullies continue to harm,
Then say your method
Of self-defense is wrong.
Nothing fucking changes
You start to believe
they never will

Dreaming in a Perfect World

They Don't Care About Us by Michael Jackson

This song was released 25 years ago, and nothing has changed black people are still unjustly incarcerated at higher rates, we're still subjected to racism at work or even when we're just minding our business. We're still dying by the hands of cops and clansmen. We've marched, rioted, and protested. Nothing works. The only thing that changes are the names we hashtag every week. My heart is heavy and numb all at once. The trauma we're subjected to is normal to us, it's almost become 2nd nature to know we could get murdered for no reason. Everyday we leave the house knowing there's a chance we may not come back, not because we're looking for trouble but because the world sees us as animals to be hunted. I just wanna know why? What did we do to deserve such treatment? Why are we hated so much. Even in peace we're killed violently. What do they want from us?

Stand With Us, Not Against

Despite being broken
by many years of trauma,
our hearts remain filled
with boundless hope,
enough to give to the brothers
and sisters who've given up

Amid the turmoil
Of illness, killing, and hatred
I pray we all
find our back to love
I pray we give each other
a shoulder to lean on
because a lot of us are aching,
May our fears wash away
So we can feel safe
to stand hand in hand again

Now is not the time
To argue 'all lives matter',
Don't protest our protest
Understand our rage
Comes from decades
of being silenced

Get out of your bubble,
open your eyes to see
the world outside of you
Listen with your heart and ears
Soak in what you don't know
So you can learn
 before you speak

85

Dreaming in a Perfect World

We're dying for our
voices to be heard
And fighting for survival
Something we've been doing
for too long

Dreaming in a Perfect World

Fighting Over Our Lives

Silence turns into violence
after decades of being unheard
Calmness turn into rage
After centuries of being hurt
We're fighting day by day
to break this curse
So, I don't know what's worse
Them trying to mute us
Or their unwillingness to learn

They say ignorance is bliss
Well, they must be in heaven
Riding their high horses, while
we get high off
2nd hand depression
My friend.
May I pose a question?
How long would you survive
If the majority
saw your skin as a weapon?

It's so easy to judge
When looking in from the outside
But we have scars on our fists
From battling for our lives
We need you to listen

Dreaming in a Perfect World

Give us a try
We're not crying just to cry
we're clawing to survive

it's your choice
to remain clueless
When it comes
to the rights of humans
There should be no confusion
So are you arguing to be obtuse
Or do you really deem us useless?

So tell me the truth
Do you care if we die?

Dreaming in a Perfect World

"Because You're Black"

I was
7 years young
At a Christian summer camp
I hated every minute of it
From the teachers shaming
Me for being left-handed
From being
one of the two and half
Black campers
To fighting every day
Because freckled-faced Billy
Despised my existence,
It felt good to kick
 his ass everyday tho,
Despite all of it all
I had one person
to look forward to AJ,
the only kid who played with me
He was white,
with a biracial sister,
one morning
Little Billy challenged me
To meet him in the bathroom,
I Did
When I showed up
He was waiting with two friends
and two sharp planks,
He tossed one to me
His friend turned off

Dreaming in a Perfect World

The light
"Let's Go" he said.
"I'm tired of fighting."
I said,
I dropped my plank,
And hurried out of the bathroom
I searched for AJ
But he wasn't around
So I asked his sister,
And she said
"He has a fever but you shouldn't
Be playing with him anyways,
because you're black"
She walked away
leaving me confused.
I isolated myself,
And ate the best
damn cheese puffs
I ever had
Until my mother arrived,
She saw my long face
Puppy dog eyes
"I don't wanna be here anymore,"
I said.
I told her about Billy,
AJ's sister,
And how horrible
my time at the camp was,
She gave those
Teachers an unpleasant
Piece of her mind,
I gathered my belongings
and never went back,
'til this day I vividly remember
The taste of those cheese puffs
And the first time I felt racism

Dreaming in a Perfect World

Dream: Old things

Sara and I traveled back to my
hometown. While take a stroll downtown
we ran into a woman I once dated, I
introduced them to eachother; the woman
Invited us to a BBQ. We went the BBQ
the weather was perfect the vibes
were right. Later that night the woman
texted me. She asked if we could meet
alone, to talk, I agreed to meet with
her without telling Sara. I arrived
at the meetup destination, which was
a rundown gas station. I waited for
a few minutes, then left.
She facetimed me, and asked "Why did you leave
I said, " You have nothing I want to hear,
there's no use in wasting my time.

Lover's Remorse

I regret falling
in love with you,
The heartache wasn't worth
losing a friend
The moment we kissed I knew
Our platonic romance would end
Nothing was the same
On you, I placed the blame
For leading me on
But it was me who came
off too strong
Or not at all
I wanted more
of your intimate love
Because I thought
Being friends
Was us settling for less
In retrospect,
Remaining friends
would've been best
I regret
falling in love with you
A line
we couldn't comeback from
I thought I would gain a lover
But losing a friend
was the outcome

Dreaming in a Perfect World

Rebirth

Sometimes goodbyes
Can be as liberating
as the first time
Air touches your soft skin
After living
Inside your mother's womb,
At first,
You may cry,
The pain may bruise,
Anxiety may travel
through your spine,
But it's alright,
Beyond all the fear
There's a bright light
Telling you,
A new life is ahead
And a thousand hellos
are ready to meet you

Monster's Ball

Monsters may come in the form of
smiles and empty promises. They say
anything that will lure hopeful hearts
into their domain. They take advantage
of innocent lovers because of the
heartaches they never healed from.

Love Circus

Love is a circus
And we've all played the clown
To please someone
We desperately
wanted to keep around

Planting in Graves

Going back to an ex
Is like trying to plant
Life in a grave
You'll find yourself
trying to save
What's already dead,
There's no way to revive
A broken foundation
Why keep chasing
after what has long evaded,
Only heartbreak
awaits on the other side
A little hope still resides
In your mind
So you keep planting
watering,
Watering
And plating
Until the dead soil
Is soaked in your tears,
You refuse to move on
Because all the years
You spent loving them
When the memories of yesterday
Were buried 6 feet deep
You were there
with your sorrows
and a shovel,
Digging to retrieve
That old feeling again
Sadly, what you had
is gone

Dreaming in a Perfect World

But If you have the strength
Love the wrong person,
You possess
the strength to move on
Leave that grave alone
find a garden,
Plant a new love

Dream # 1   Dementia

My thoughts were scattered. I couldn't remember what I was doing and why I was doing it. Every other sentence was "oh I forgot." everything was cloudy. As i reached Into a the cabinet, and stand blankly. Sara asked "What are you doing", My response was "I dont know". The simple things we take for granted became a Frustrating task Walking, sitting, eating. Absolutely nothing made sense.

My body became stiff and useless, I lost all sense of awareness. I was a Shell of myself

Dreaming in a Perfect World

Like Sand in an Hourglass

The old man
sits still,
Staring at the wall
With an upside down spoon
In his hands,
His food is getting cold,
But he doesn't know

The old man
sits in his recliner
With a slipper to his ear,
Laughing out loud
At a joke
Said by a friend
Who no longer exists

The old man
Sits in his shower chair,
Unaware of where he is
Until warm pellets of water
Hits his liver spotted skin
"Stop it" he screams,
with grave fear in his eyes.

The old man gazes
Into the mirror
And plays the guessing game
At his reflection
A game he never wins

Dreaming in a Perfect World

"Damn" I say to the old man
As my tongue fumble the words
I wish I could say
But I know he wouldn't understand,
I shake my head,
He stares at me
Like I'm a ghost

I've witnessed death
in many forms
But none have shattered
my heart more than
Seeing a man's mind wither away
Like sand in an hourglass,
Grain by Grain,
His memories slowly slip away
Until his time expires.
Dementia is the bastard child
of father time

*Dedicated to my friend William Lewis. A
group home resident I've gotten the
pleasure to know.*

A Poem About Forgetting You

Sometimes,
I wish the memory of you
Would fade away
like sand in the wind,

Sometimes, I wish
Your name would feel
like a foreign word
rolling off the tip of my tongue

Sometimes, I wish I could
Go back in time
So I could turn the other way
When your eyes found mine

Then there are other times
I'm happy,
the bitter memories of you
still lives in my brain

you taught me
what my heart deserved
when I was too naïve to believe
it wouldn't beat for anyone else

Because of you I learned
How to appreciate heartache

Cancel Culture is a Joke

Cancel culture transformed from a
movement that made celebs and
influencers accountable for their
inappropriate actions while giving them
space to grow, to a running joke. It
has become a Pro-bullying movement
where all offenses are treated with the
same punishment. Distasteful jokes from
ten years ago get cast in the same
bubble as racist and perverted
behaviors, of today. The cancel culture
vultures carry themselves like they're
the circle of perfect people who've
never made a mistake or made a bad
joke. Have they forgotten they're
humans too? Who the fuck made them God?

Cancel culture is a joke; they tweet
about how mental health is essential
then quickly bombard a celebrity for
saying something out of line.

Dreaming in a Perfect World

Cancel culture vultures bully with
misinformed narratives after reading
one headline from a faux-article. They
react before doing research, but
they're so perfect, right? Dementia
must stricken the part of the brain
that controls their empathy, but they
don't give a damn about how a celeb's
mental health when they attack their
appearance or family over a tweet that
was taken out of context. Who controls
these vultures? Who holds cancel
culture accountable when they screw up?
They don't know, they must've forgotten
that famous people are humans too.

Dreaming in a Perfect World

Dream ≠ Death

I recieved the news from my Mom that my sister died. My heart was shattered and I couldnt even breathe. I tried to move but my body was still. I didnt understand. A Part of me died and I couldnt no longer wanted to live

Angels Going Home

Just the thought of losing
Someone I love
Brings a storm to my eyes
I know it's inevitable
But I'll never be ready to see
Any of them die

Chill bumps cover my skin
Like I'm nude amid winter wind
When I ponder the last time
I see them again

I overthink myself
Into spell of anxiety
Drunk off fear
Crying for sobriety
I pray to the sky
They never die on me

I know one day
God will call his angels home
But my greatest fear
Is living on earth alone

The Haunting

Passing through Northern Florida,
There was a white house
of rotted wood,
Surrounded by a mile
of brown grass,
And a few cabins nearby,
My first sighting of a slave
plantation,
My eyes welled
and heart swelled
With horror and sadness
Time tortured me,
By slowing down
Forcing me to feel
The spirits that haunted
The plain,
I thought about
the blood on the leaves
What if that blood
had belonged to me?
The echoes of slave cries
and hymns
Rang my ears,
My body shivered with chills
In a flash,
I saw the reality of a slave
What they called home
Was actually a grave

Honor The Dead

When a loved one dies
We tend to take a possession
they left behind
And hold onto it
for dear life
finding comfort
in their coffee mug,
Snug in ragged blankets
For the warmth of their hug,
Wearing their
favorite band shirts
To feel less hurt,
Or walking in their Nikes
To feel what it was like
to walk a mile in their life
We take these cheap tools
And turn them
in to priceless jewels
Holding them on
'til the last thread
This is how we honor the dead

Dreaming in a Perfect World

A Typical Day As an 8-year-old boy in the Hood

His body
Laid on the hot bed of grass
Like he was sunbathing
My mother demanded me
to cover my eyes
But my childish curiosity
Defied her wishes,
My eyes narrowed
On the brown man
With dark red Kool-Aid stains
On his holy shirt
"Why would he take a nap
Outside like that?"
"Why my cousins and
Uncles just staring at him?"
I thought to myself
The cops cars arrived
"Maybe they're coming
to wake him up,"

Dreaming in a Perfect World

I thought.
The red and white truck
With its blaring siren
And dizzy lights
came speeding down
The brick road.
They put him on a flat mattress
"are they putting him to bed?"
I asked my mom
as they pulled the white sheet
over his face.
"No baby, he won't be waking up
anytime soon" she said.

When Good People Die

When you die your soul leaves from your
retired body to find a new home in a
new vessel, and all the lessons you
learned and the pain you suffered from
during your past life becomes
intuition. You feel things before you
see them, because your soul has been
there before. As eternity moves on your
soul travels from body to body,
collecting new memories and
perspectives. Maybe your empathy runs
deep because you've lived a thousand
different lives already.

Dreaming in a Perfect World

The land was scarce of plants and trees.
No sight of wild life was near. Myself, sara,
and my family traveled on Foxx, in hopes
of finding any sign of life. There was
a book I held. The book flew out of my
hands and we chased It. We were
led to an unclear space. A plant bloomed
a few flowers too. Tree grew as tall
as Skyscrapers, and birds flocked.
We marveled at the sight of
new beginnings.

Dreaming in a Perfect World

Our Burning Land

Sometimes a Forrest must burn
For stronger trees
to emerge from fresh soil,
You see chaos
But I see rebirth,
As wild embers climb
to the sky
Made of orange sparks
and smoke
you see devastation,
But I see growth
As trees and plants
Slowly erode
clouds of smoke
Loom over the animal's home,
You feel a loss
I feel new hope,
Once the smoke clears
Then comes the rain
just like nature
we conjure flames
So we can enforce change
You think it's absurd,
It's our way
of burning the pain

New History

Since age five,
Everything we were taught
From white Jesus
to Christopher Columbus
Was a lie
How am I supposed to believe,
Dinosaurs were alive?
So why honor Christmas,
Thanksgiving
Or the 4th of July?
When the history
they want us to celebrate
was built from bloodshed
of the innocent
and coldhearted hate,
but they want us to wait
'til we die for things to change,
No longer, we will sit idly
To their empty promises
We will break these shackles
And ascend
to a higher consciousness
It's obvious,
The truth they
didn't want us to learn
that's why the statues must go,
the history books must burn,
so we can rewrite history,
the history we deserve.

Little Fires Everywhere

When the life
you're used to,
slowly comes to
a blazing end
stand brave
amid the hurricane
of flames,
don't run away
Claim your land
You may not understand
In the moment
Why everything you love
is burning to dust
But you must trust
Better days are ahead.
And chaos won't last forever
Sometimes, what you've built
must catch fire
to inspire you to
pursue the life
you always desired.

Happiness hits different

Happiness hits different when you focus
on watering the grass you were given
without competing with your neighbors
to see whose lawn is greener. Beauty
takes time; growth can't be rushed.
Take pride in what you have and put in
the work to see it flourish. Other
grass may be greener, but what you have
is a blessing you were given.

Ain't Nothing Sweet About This

I wish I could write something with an optimistic tone about how 2020 is the year for growth and clarity. Unfortunately, those words don't exist. Reality is too dark to see the silver lining. People are dying at the hands of racism and a virus. Cops stopped being protectors and turned into hunters. Children are being prostituted and molested by sick fucks in Hollywood and Congress. Our natural resources are tainted by toxins. This world has become a playground for demons. Sadly, none of these pandemics are new, and if this year is your 'awakening,' congrats, because a lot of us were not afforded the luxury of living in blissful ignorance. Many of us, were forced into this reality before we could recite the alphabet. So, I'm sorry for not writing inspirational prose to massage your discomfort. I don't know what the fuck is going on or what's going to happen next. I'm scared, tired, and emotionally drained, but I still believe in love. I still have hope. I feel a change coming, I just hope I'm alive for it.

Dreaming in a Perfect World

To the White man who calls me Brotha
Vs the white man who doesn't see color

When you call me brotha
You're saying
You acknowledge my blackness
My blackness provides comfort
in your space
My blackness doesn't make
you feel insecure
My blackness doesn't anger you
My blackness
is seen and appreciated
My blackness
is a source of love and light
By calling me brotha
You're presenting yourself
As an ally I can trust
An ally I can embrace
with a hug and a handshake

when you say
"I don't see color."
In any context,
You're saying,
You choose to be blind
And willfully ignorant
You're saying my blackness
Isn't worthy
of a healthy conversation
My blackness
makes you check your pockets
for your wallet

Dreaming in a Perfect World

My blackness
makes you upset
My blackness
is an exaggerated plight
And your privilege doesn't exist
Most of all when you say
"I don't see color"
With such conviction
You're saying
You don't see me,
And that's the fucking problem

The Blooming

Flowers rarely bloom
after the first sunset
or break after
the first storm
So be patient
with your healing
The way nature
Is with her flowers
Beauty takes time to flourish

Dreaming in a Perfect World

Dreamy: The Deadbeat

I was at my mom's house eating cereal. My sister, her son, and baby daddy were on the couch. Micah (her son) began to cry. He tried to snatch him from her arms. When she refused he yelled "you acting like a bitch" I rushed to her side and stepped to him. I said "Look, you ain't shit, and you dont run shi- he stood up and said "Fuck you," he pushed me. I punched him so hard his chin left an imprint on the wall. He fell to the floor. I hate deadbeat dads.

Dreaming in a Perfect World

"How does a deadbeat sleep well at
night knowing they have a child
yearning for their love? They're
probably dead inside, that's why.'

Stream of Consciousness III

I refuse to associate myself with
deadbeat fathers because I will
constantly remind them of how much of a
loser they are. A day wouldn't go by
without me shaming them for being a
shitty human. Most deadbeats punish
their children despite the mother,
others are just cowards running away
from their responsibilities. No matter
what, there's no excuse to desert your
seed, and that's why deadbeats have no
place in my life in any capacity,

Dreaming in a Perfect World

Dream to Come

I created a tiktok of me dancing to my song "Lowrider Spaceship". The video went viral, teens worldwide used my sounds. Charlie D'amelio posted a video, then my song flew up the charts on itunes. In one hour my life changed. Soon after I was on talk shows, gained millions of followers, invited to celeb events. I thought I was living the dream, until I had a mental breakdown. I couldn't handle the pressure and I folded. I became a recluse. I learned that even if you chase something it may not be good for you.

Blame TMZ

The fact celebs feel compelled to
explain their relationships to the
public shows how unhealthy the fan-
celebrity dynamic is. We shouldn't be
so invested in their personal lives.
The media created this celeb obsession,
which gave us the entitlement to pry
into their lives.

Dreaming in a Perfect World

For All Mindless Entertainment

Today's youth is so
Thirsty for fame
they'll do anything
to quench their thirst
the viral addiction
of attention
has a generation
performing mindless acts
to receive their next high
So programmed and strung out
Controlled by retweets and likes
They're willing to jeopardize
their life
To impress strangers.
Constantly chasing validation,
They no longer have minds
of their own
hopping on every trend
following every false narrative
They're just that desperate
To have a voice,
They're itching to be famous
For all the wrong reasons
Slaves to social media
The new-age digital fiends

Dream # Gum

I was standing by a gate. My friends
were on the other side. As I was
chewing on bubble gum and tried to spit
it out. The became too ~~too~~ sticky to
spit out so I attempted take it out
with my hand. The gum expanded & thickened,
The more I tried to discard the gum the
bigger the wad grew. After awhile
my entire body was covered in gum.
I was stuck in my own mess,
trying to fix it alone.

Summer Sadness

Today,
I feel like shit,
My mind is a battlefield
Where my thoughts
Are At war,
Trying to
Kill each other off
Until sadness calls truce
I want to cry,
But my tears have
too much pride
To show their truth
My bed is the only place
I wish to be
But the sun
Is too stubborn to let me
Dwell in darkness
Today, I want to be heartless,
Feel nothing
But something more powerful
is telling me
to keep flowing
Like a cool blue river
So, I take each moment in
by the minute
And let love rejuvenate me
Today is not my day,

Dreaming in a Perfect World

and that's okay
I'll make the best of it
Instead of wallowing
in my own pity

Dreaming in a Perfect World

A word

You only say I'm emotional
as an insult when you lack
the intellectual depth to innerstand
me.

Dreaming in a Perfect World

Black Student, White Teacher

Imagine,
It's the first week of February'
You're one of the few
specs of pepper
in a class of salt,
The walls are taped
With posters of
famous black figures
That reads
Happy Black History Month
In the middle,
Your teacher
Greets you
With her tar stained smile
Then stares
Until wrinkles
become waves above her 'brows
"Open your Books"
She tells the class
You turn to the small
section dedicated
To sisters and brethren of melanin,
It begins with slavery,
The whippings, the chains
the rapes,

Dreaming in a Perfect World

images of Fredrick Douglas
And Harriet Tubman
To symbolize perseverance
Next to a larger photo of
the white savior
Abe Lincoln,
to prove
not all whites were bad
The next page,
"Jim Crow" and "Civil Rights"
The hosings,
Dog bitings,
burning houses,
bodies dangling from trees,
blood on the leaves
white ghosts on horses,
Rosa Parks and boycotts,
You all recite small bits from
Martin Luther's dream
but never learn the full speech,
You receive a mix of stares
From the white students

Some snicker, others pity
When it's your turn
to read aloud.
Then you all

Dreaming in a Perfect World

get assigned to write
about your favorite black hero.
The White kids look to you
to be the beacon
of black knowledge
Sadly, you know
as much as they do

And that's the reality of
black history month
For most black students,
Our history summed up
in one chapter
While Christopher Columbus
Gets praised like a hero
for a semester
They teach us about our trauma
But don't spend
a second on our heritage,
Our customs or language
They brainwashed us to believe
That slavery is our identity
And getting lynched
Is our culture

Dreaming in a Perfect World

Dream #9

My friends Tim and MJay, and I were
walking through the park. A raccoon
leaped from a tree into the lake. MJay
was so impressed he followed the raccoon.
The raccoon jumped out the water
and into the tree, he then jumped from
tree to tree. MJay and Tim followed
the raccoon as I went the opposite
direction. I saw a bright orange & white
fox. I climbed a tree to remain close.
The fox ran away. Another fox appeared
and leaped into the tree. I leaped off
the tree and ran away. Another
fox appeared from behind a tree
and bit my arm. As my arm swelled, I reached
out to pet him. Tim and MJay found
me surrounded by a pack of foxes, but
I was happy and relaxed.

Lost in Yesterday

My impulsiveness
gets the best of me
when these raw emotions
tangle with my logic
and win

I often react too fast
And say things
I can't beg time
To take back

I've fumbled
good opportunities
Off my trembling hands
By overthinking
'til the sun
kissed me goodnight

I try so hard
to control my mind
But I jump to conclusions
Like a skydiver
With a broke 'chute.

I try my best
To assess and react less
But impulsiveness
Likes to play tricks on me

Dreaming in a Perfect World

Once Upon a Friend

I once had a friend
Who came from a troubled home,
We would go to teen parties
I paid his way
And made sure
he ate when I did.
When he needed money
My uncle let him sweep and clean
At his barbershop
When his mother locked him out
my father let him sleepover
'til the scent of pancakes
And bacon traveled
To our nostrils.
Sometimes I woke up
with less money
in my wallet than
I fell asleep with
"Maybe I spent it,"
"Maybe I lost it,"
"Maybe I miscounted,"
Were excuses I created,
As he stared at me dumbfoundedly.
One day,
he came over
Wearing a shirt too expensive

Dreaming in a Perfect World

for a barbershop
sweeper salary.
He bragged
And I questioned
"I've been saving." he said
I knew he was lying
But I continued
to be his friend
Out of pity.
From him, I learned
No matter how good
of a friend you are
some people will find a way
steal your goodwill
swifter than a fox creeping
under a full moon

Dreaming in a Perfect World

Dream - Driving Into Water

My friend Jamal was driving with with
Me and Johnny on the hood. Jamal got
Lost and drove into a body of water.
As the vehicle was submerged we managed
to was walk out of the water. Once
we reached the surface
our clothes were dry. We continued
proceeded to our destination on foot.

She Is Most Powerful

She is most powerful
when given space
To freely express
Every dimension
of her existence

She is most powerful
When the weight
of perfection
Isn't holding her down,
Giving her the courage
to live fearlessly.

She is most powerful
When she isn't being held back
From her fruitful future
By toxic love

she is most powerful
When her wisdom
Can plant seeds
in fresh soil
Instead of her tears

So leave her alone if
You are incapable
Of adding beauty
to her light
She doesn't need
any darkness in her life

Dreaming in a Perfect World

Things black people should stop saying to other black People

nigga. Overused and gentrified. Even as a term of endearment it still sounds crude and caging. Something we claim to be empowering is often interchanged as an insult. We've outgrown the word. There's no room left for the nword in this new resurgence of black pride. Let's detach from the word. We're royalty now.

You're not "black-black", what makes someone's blackness less valid than the next? Maybe your background is different but most things remain the same outside of your four walls. Going outside is like playing Russian Roulette for any black person. Their complexion doesn't protect them from being hunted by American terrorists. Trayvon and Emmitt's fairer skin did not save them. Remember All black is beautiful, all black is valid, and all black is worthy of equal respect.

Dreaming in a Perfect World

"You can't date outside your race and be pro-black". This mindset was once valid but now outdated. The heart doesn't choose who to fall in love with, love finds us. Love holds no bounds. Love doesn't discriminate. As long as a black person fights for and with brothers and sisters while educating their spouse, the color of the person their with shouldn't be seen as a disqualifier. Besides we know a lot of modern-day Uncle Toms tap dancing for white approval and coming home to their black spouse. In the end, the color of our spouse shouldn't matter; our actions should.

Dreaming in a Perfect World

"We got a lot of unlearning and Self-
healing to do. Time to put in the
work."

Dreaming in a Perfect World

Emotional Surfing

Surfing through
Waves of emotions
Trying to stay afloat
I gotta remain patient
Never lose hope
Soon these emotions
will settle
And the waves will erode
As I continue to go
I will find my way
To shore

Dreaming in a Perfect World

Dream # 8 comparisons

I posted a poem to tiktok one evening
a young woman ☐ said, "You're no Whitman."
Moments later a young man ☐ commented
"He's no Bukowski, either"
My agitation grew and wrote to them
"Yes, I am a young black man, and
they are two dead white men so you're
correct."

Later on Instagram someone wrote to
to say, "You're no Rh Sin". This pissed
me off the most. I told her,
"Thank you, because I would never try
to profit off ☐ women's trauma".

Soon after someone said, "You remind
me of Atticus". ☐☐☐ I cringed and
said, "I don't have to wear a mask, because
I'm not ashamed of my truth."

☐☐ Theres nothing I hate more than
being compared.

Feeling Unpretty

You stare into the mirror
And see the image of
someone you admire
But it's not you

You double tap photos
That have been manipulated
Through apps for aesthetics
And dream of having
Their body and perfect skin

You compare
Your existence
To a figment
Of an unrealistic image
And fall in love
With mirages and facades

Endlessly feeling unpretty
Every time you see
breasts larger
skin clearer,
abs more defined,
Waists smaller,
Or
Shoulders more buff,
Than yours

You find yourself chasing
After beautiful lies,
Because the people
You compare yourself

Dreaming in a Perfect World

To are running
Away from their
insecurities too

Find the beauty
Within you
Without trying to fit
In someone else's shoes

Dreaming in a Perfect World

A Break from Black Excellence

Why do I have
to be excellent get noticed?
Why must I be perfect
to feel worthy
Some days I wish
I had the luxury
Of being mediocre
like Gabbie Hannah
I wish I had the space
to be average
Like the Shane Dawson
Why must I be flawless
To feel loved?
Who do I have
to be original
to be respected?
Why can't I recycle shit
Like those corny TikTok dances

Somedays I want to wake up
And go half-assed
And get double the praise
But I gotta work
Twice as hard
to get half my worth

Dreaming in a Perfect World

Somedays I wish
I could be
a watered down
version of myself
Why must I be Denzel
Every time I perform?
Why can't I be
the stars of Twilight
And get paid for it

Being excellent is exhausting
I wish I could be mediocre
For only a few moments

Dreaming in a Perfect World

Pain for Profit

Drink some tummy tea
to make your stomach
look flat like a canvass
even though
 it will make you shit
like a ferret
you'll always feel lightheaded
but it's worth it right?

Wear Organ crushing
waist trainers
to achieve
an hour glass figure
you'll suffocate your lungs
you may pass out
but your waistline
will be to die for

Swallow those supplements
That'll will make your dick
Shrivel like shrimp
But it's fine
Because the social media
compliments compensates
for what you can't do in bed

Dreaming in a Perfect World

But this isn't your fault,
Your insecurities are targeted
For marketing
Brands pay your favorite
influencers and celebs
Thousands of dollars
for a photo op

Telling you to *BUY BUY BUY*
Pretending this product is why
Their body is perfect
Making you feel worthless

In reality, they don't drink
The shitty tummy tea
Or pop those steroid pills
Or use the waist trainers,
But they're using you.

to sell to your insecurities
and your irrational
desire to be perfect,

They Profit off
your desire
to look like
your favorite celebrity
This is why
Body image
is a billion-dollar industry

"The Perfect Black Man"

"You're so well-spoken"
They say
with their eyes wide open
Like they're shocked
to see a black person
Speak with such clarity.
Which insinuates
every white person
Speaks like a dictionary
"You're Not Black-Black"
They say in reference
to my skin tone
Or personality
Suggesting my fairer skin
is more approachable
or demeanor makes
me more acceptable
Like I give a fuck about
Making them more comfortable
with their closeted racism
They paint me
as their definition
of a perfect black man
The
"I'll let you date my daughter" type
The
"you're not like the rest"
type

Dreaming in a Perfect World

To distinguish me
from my skinfolk
Like I'm supposed to be proud
To have their validation
I laugh out loud
When they think
it's okay
to compliment me
for not fitting inside
the stereotype
they assumed me to be
They can keep the bullshit
I ain't buying

Dreaming in a Perfect World

Dream, floating

I was floating in air. I felt like a bird.
Having the ability to launch from the
ground, into air was so liberating.
Since I Driving was never my forte.
I found profound comfort traveling
through air.

Life on Autopilot

Sometimes,
I wish I could float
through life,
coast on autopilot.

Somedays,
I wish days
Life was
easy like Sunday morning
With Lionel Richie
Singing on the porch

Everything worth loving
Comes with a struggle
if it comes easy
It's worth nothing

Living in this paradox
Wish I could detox from
all the suffering
my heart has gone through

My poor little heart
Deserves a break
from worrying so much
I wish I could float
Through my days
carefree and blissfully

Dreaming in a Perfect World

Stream of Consciousness IV

I dream in HD
When life feels
Too dim to see,
Everyday I feel
the weight of the world
anchoring my feet
but when I drift into a dream
my wings become free
Reality is a burden
I escape
When I float in my dreams
With the clouds
beneath my feet
I am an infinite being
Skipping on Saturn's ring
I am the best version of me
when I sleep
cause my heart
is void of anxiety
I breath in peace
And exhale bliss
With my eyes closed
The real world
is something
I don't miss

Dreaming in a Perfect World

"Before you go to sleep, apologize to
the universe for the times you
neglected your blessings because you
were too busy complaining about what
you didn't have."

Dreaming in a Perfect World

All Lives Matter

If all lives truly
Matter to you
You'd fight with me
Not against me.

Dreaming in a Perfect World

Dream: The argument

My Mother and I were clashing verbally.
She was yelling from the bottom of her
heart. I said things I could never come back
From. I have no clue why were arguing.
My belongings were packed in a trashbag.
My sisters were crying as I storm
Stormed out of the house. It was broad
daylight. I walked the trail as
the sun burnt the pback of my neck.
I cried, and my heart was broken.
No amount of apologies would've fix
what happened

Dreaming in a Perfect World

"Sitting back and observing is less
stressful than trying to get my point
across to stubborn people."

Dreaming in a Perfect World

Floating away

As I grow older
I've realized
Some situations
Don't need to be fixed
And it's best
to float away
Than to stay,
maintaining my peace
is more important
Than getting my point across.
Some people are committed
to judging you
And others are dedicated
to misunderstanding you
and no amount of truth
will change their
perception of you
That's why I've found peace
In drifting away from the people
Who refuse to accept my growth
When I casually float out
of their life
They find themselves reaching
For my presence to come back.
Once I ascend
Too high into the sky
There's no coming back

Loveless Marriage

My first heartbreak
was the moment I realized
my parents weren't perfect
The two figures who appeared
larger than life, immortal even,
suddenly became human,
and the golden frame
I placed
their perfect image in
was shattered.
Shards of the life
I thought we once had
got scattered all over the tile.
After years of fighting, cursing,
And living in a frozen home
From months of giving each other
the cold shoulder
Their vows ran its course
They finally said
"son, we're getting a divorce"
I was relieved
We didn't have to pretend
Everything was fine anymore

The Mother vs The Child II

She yelled words that
Felt like a sword
Piercing through my core,
It was time to leave home
at that moment l knew
The hands of time
were telling me to move on
I was getting older
I had to move forward
Sometimes it's hard
for a mother to let go
But as long
I was under her roof
There was no space to grow,
Is what I told her
As my cloudy eyes began to pour,
Our home became a thunderstorm
Unsure of how we'd go
back to our sunny days
I packed my things,
And asked a friend if
I could stay at his place,
But I had to wait,
I sat in my room

Dreaming in a Perfect World

Til the daylight said goodbye,
Hoping she'll swallow her pride
And apologize
To my surprise
She said
"what do you want
to eat tonight?"

"Pizza"
She said "all right."
I knew that was the
end of our fight
And the closest thing
to "I'm sorry"
She had given in a while

Dreaming in a Perfect World

Good parents are never perfect and
perfect parents don't exist.

They're deeply flawed artists
trying to craft a masterpiece
onto a blank canvass
with no experience
and a raggedy paint brush
they inherited
from their parents,
They spend sleepless nights
And tireless hours
painting patterns, hues,
and dimensions onto you,
there's no outline or plan,
so they make mistakes
they can't erase
along the way,
they just paint,
because each stroke
of the brush
is a new lesson
you'll acquire,
They only get better
with time,
While working a 9-5
Then come home tired
to an endless job,
Being an artist is hard
That comes with an impossible

Dreaming in a Perfect World

Pressure to live up to,
So don't hold grudges
For their mistakes
They tried their best,
Good parents are never perfect
And perfect parents don't exist,
If you grew up
a decent human
Then the art they created
Is a success

Dreaming in a Perfect World

Dream: Kobe

Sitting And the darkness, self-Doubt began to
break my [illegible] mind by Storm. [illegible]
My Mind led me to believe My [illegible] Art
[illegible] wasn't good enough. Kobe's ghost
appeared. He watched as I wallowed and
[illegible] said "STop playing your self".
I stared in shock and confusion.
"You got this youre wasting time doubting
yourself. Keep writing". He answered, and
faded away. My heart was pounding. I picked
up a pen & a pad and began writing

Dreaming in a Perfect World

Dear Kobe,

You were a part
of many holidays,
BBQs and black barbershop debates
Friendships were made
because of you,
For 20 years
We watched you create
timeless memories
in three second flashes.
'Clutch time' became 'Kobe time'
The aerodynamic dunks,
the silky smooth fadeaways,
left us all amazed
Black children worldwide
Let their hair grow
into nappy fros
Shouting 'Kobe'
For every jumper at the park
Or every paper ball shot in the
classroom.
Your name became
synonymous with a culture
Of excellence
The smile
The drive
The style
The work ethic
The passion
the action

Dreaming in a Perfect World

You inspired
Children like myself
To do what I do
Until the day
I cease to breathe
I'll never forget
what you taught me
Thank you, Kobe
For leaving it all on the court

Dreaming in a Perfect World

Dream: Ghosting

I was at a KMart, which was sort of strange
because those hardly exist anymore. I ran
into this girl I used to "talk to". She pretended
not to see me until I said "hey remember me"
She yelled "no" and called me a "Faggot".
Her best friend grabbed her, I followed them
out. I asked how she been, but she
responded with, "why'd you stopped talking
to me?", I said "I was in a bad place, sorry.
I told her about my current space in life
how I found love, moved to a new state.
She stared with half of a smile on her face.

"Well it was nice seeing you" she said
but her tome wasn't pleasant. She got
into her friend's car. Rain suddenly
poured onto me, only me.

168

A Heartbreak Theory

Some people like to believe they can
change, but the people who hurt them
can't. that's a selfish way to think.
Everyone deserves a chance to learn
and grow from the pain they caused.
Everyone who hurts you isn't a bad
person, maybe they weren't mature
enough or ready to commit. Some are in
love with the idea of love, but not
ready to put in the work. If you can
grow from your mistakes, they can as
well.

Ambition

Her drive attracts attention
From people who want
to join the ride
if you aren't willing
to add fuel
to her engine
don't interrupt her journey
watch her travel
and admire her ambition

Dreaming in a Perfect World

"Sometimes broken promises come from
the sweetest lips."

Dream # 6 "Cheating"

The state governor announced that the state was going into full lock down. No one going in or out. My coworker and I were stuck at work for 3 days straight. My coworker announced told me she was getting She hugged them me and quickly kissed my lips. I pushed her away. She pulled her pants down.

"You dont have to tell her? She said. hant over the could I gave in. We had sex in silence, trying not to wake the residence.

the next day Sara and I were at a party. the guilt quickly began to eat me alive.

"whats wrong?" She asked. I kept fumbling items and pacing around. She saw the troubled look on my face. Her eyes began to worry.

" I slept with someone." I tried, breaking down piece by piece.

Dreaming in a Perfect World

Something I Must Promise

Being loved by you is a privilege, so I
handle your heart with care. I wouldn't
dare to inflict pain onto your heart
and ethereal soul. The smile in your
eyes when you say *you love me* sends
bliss passing through my soul, so why
would I ever drag you through hell? My
loyalty will never lose to temptation.
Your trust will never be deceived by
pretty lies, My entire being is devoted
to making sure happiness ignites those
ebony eyes, every time I cross your
mind. Home feels like heaven because
love lives with us. A broken home our
haven will never become, I'm all yours,
baby.

Dreaming in a Perfect World

"Find a love that doesn't kill you
But takes your breath away."

Dreaming in a Perfect World

This is for You

The wrong love will make
you feel so lost,
your reflection becomes
a stranger,
When you stare wondering
How you've managed to travel
so far away from
Who you used to be
You blame yourself
for not being enough,
You question your heart
Desperate for answers,
you get nothing in return,
You're not happy
it's in plain sight
But you think
It's a patch you
Two can sow together
So, you continue to
swallow your pride
Like pills and wine
Intoxicating yourself
with their lies.
Hoping for a change
The rough patch remains
And the love
you two once shared
Is a one-sided fantasy
You allowed this person
To take you so far away
from who you are
You become a distant shadow

Dreaming in a Perfect World

In the rearview
You've somehow built up
the strength to
love this person
Why can't you cultivate
that same energy to leave
what's hurting you?

Gaslight, Gaslight

They try to hold on long after you let
go, without realizing your loyalty led
you to looking foolish over them. The
moment you run out of chances to spare,
they pretend to care, and remake the
promises they broke over and over.
After breaking your heart in countless
ways, they beg you to stay one more
day. When tears storm from your cloudy
eyes, they bring up the sunny days to
down bring your guard down. They
manipulate their way back into your
good graces. This is what happens when
you fall in love with a narcissistic
gaslighter.

Dreaming in a Perfect World

The Vulnerable Man

Every man doesn't
Love from behind a brick wall
not every man heart is
made of stone,
and when you find a man
Who wears his emotion
On a sleeve
Listen to him
Without invalidating
His feelings
Listen without trying
to suppress
His feelings
Men deserve compassion too,

She Cant Always Revive Everything

Don't wait until silence
becomes her language
to finally listen
to her voice.

Don't wait
until she walks away
to finally hold her close

Don't wait for her
Eyes to rain
to promise
Brighter days

don't wait 'til
She walks away
To realize
 she's your everything

Dreaming in a Perfect World

Dream: falling In Love

We, Sara & I were bathing in the sun on an exotic beach. We swam in a Jacuzzi, in a fancy hotel room. We traveled from destination to destination, exploring the world together.

Cant wait for this dream to become reality

Dreaming in a Perfect World

Anniversary

Two years down,
forever more to go
With you,
We envisioned these moments
From daydreams
and pillow thoughts
Now we celebrate
The reality of this love
we invented,
with confetti on the mattress,
and burning scented candles
in the air
while my fingers
tangle in your hair
Our anniversary,
A holiday honoring you and I
The stars are gonna'
 clap for us
As we bask in our passion
Magic will rain down
On our love
Forever more
I'm so eager
to grow old with you
I just hope time
doesn't fly
Too fast

Sunrise Smiles

When her smile rises
like the morning sun
My entire world forgets
what it feels like to be dark

Dreaming in a Perfect World

Three Words

We say "*I Love You.*"
every time
We cross each other's
mind
'cuz when we die
Our souls
will rest easy
Knowing we left this earth
Without an "I love you."
Unsaid

The Rich Man

I once heard
"Words lose value over time."
So why does
my soul feel richer
Every time
"I love you."
Travels from her lips
to my mind?
'cuz true love is priceless
And I'll never go broke
For as long
as she loves me

Dreaming in a Perfect World

On Key

When the rhythm of my heart
Dances like
it has two left feet
She meets me
where it hurts
To serenade my soul
With joy and laughter
Soon after,
My heart finds itself
Dancing to the right key,
again

Heaven

If heaven were a place
My head could rest
It would be the space
Between your heart and mind

Dreaming in a Perfect World

Dream #5 - Issues

Sara and I took a 3am drive. ~~Since~~ She refused ~~to tell~~ ~~me~~ where we were going, so I was along with it. ~~An~~ She parc parked in front of this old mansion.

"I think it's ~~Dad~~ ~~out~~ get away fine and I agreed." I ~~questioned~~ ~~asked~~ her. She showed me around. There was a ~~box~~ box with written ~~letters~~ letters Scattered all over. One was from an old friend of hers. I got ~~so~~ jealous when ~~this~~ ~~I saw~~ ~~this~~ "Love ~~that~~ the gives a Sara ~~Sara~~ explained it was nothing ~~to~~ worry about. We ~~had~~ lied in bed. She answered a ~~face time~~ call from a guy I ~~never~~ seen. He expressed his ~~awareness~~ and ~~invited~~ her to a basketball game. I ~~kissed~~ ~~her~~ Sucked her neck and rubbed her breasts. She ended the call and we made ~~out~~. The next morning her father told her ~~a~~ ~~secret~~ only I knew. She stormed off ~~in the morning~~. Before the day trying to ~~get~~ talk to her. She arrived ~~back~~, ~~at the time~~ with a best friend, he told me, they were on a date. I told him to "fuck off". We ~~had to~~ ~~talk~~ and talked for hours ~~about how~~ miserable we were apart. The ~~apologies~~ ~~they~~ were ~~said~~ ~~and~~ ~~we~~ ~~finally~~ ~~realize~~

Dreaming in a Perfect World

Summer Snow

Summer snow,
Where would I go
without you home
Life without you
Would feel like
The sun without warmth

My summer snow,
Falling from the sky
So peacefully
In mid-July,
I would die
If your smile
ever fades
from the sight
Of my eyes

Summer snow,
Sprinkling from heaven
My 11:11
Every wish comes true
Your love is a blessing
You came into my life
When I least expected

The (un)truth about Magic

Lies are like magic tricks,
They create illusions to the
heart and eyes,
tangible enough for hopeful
minds to believe
and mysterious enough
to keep hopeful hearts intrigued

Fake Belief

We seem to fall for liars and
question the real ones. Why?
Maybe, because liars tell us what we
want to hear, to make us feel good,
so they can get what they want.
While the honest people
Say what we truly feel
But afraid to accept
The truth hurts
And lies brings fake bliss

Dreaming in a Perfect World

The Babies

Moon & I had two babies.
One the size of a watermelon,
the other the size of a peanut. She was
holding the watermelon sized baby
who was crying incessantly. I was
tending to the peanut sized baby
. She was laughing as I tickled
her. She slowly began to expand
until she reached the ceiling.
Soothed the big baby until she fell asleep

Dreaming in a Perfect World

Fathering

The thought of
having a little one
sends sparks flying
through my imagination
and butterflies rushing
through my stomach.
I think about sing-a-longs
on car rides from school
or saving them from
the boogey man at night.
I dream of sipping imaginary tea
And eating a slice of
the cake they baked
from thin air
on the other end,
I think about
Giving my all
And still not being enough,
I fear not being available
To play all the time
Because I'd be too busy
Working two 9-5s
I fear disappointing my child
Too many times,

Dreaming in a Perfect World

I just want to be
My child's hero
The joy and anxiety
Of bringing life
into this world
Keeps me up sometimes
Some days I'm ready
to have one
Some days I'm not,

No matter what,
When my baby stares
Into daddy's eyes
They will know I'll be there
Through thick and thin
And My love
will never be conditional

Dreaming in a Perfect World

<u>To my Unborn Child</u>

you will never have to live
a day in fear,
My heart is your safe space
to be you, unapologetically
I promise
You will never feel
out of place
In your own home
The world
is already cruel enough

Dreaming in a Perfect World

Dream: Losing Her

We were relaxing, and watching a movie.
Sara suddenly got up and dressed.
Where are you going? I asked.
She left without saying a word. For a few
hours I didn't worry. Darkness fell — I texted
her, called her family. No one knew
anything. She didn't answer my calls.
I visited every place I knew, and her friend's
house. She was gone. I cried screaming
outside, on the pavement.

Eternity

Your soul will never
Feel lonely again
I will pour every ounce of
My love to you
For eternity and more

Dreaming in a Perfect World

New Home

Sadness got evicted

the moment your love

made my heart a home

Happiness is a Home

Happiness is our home
And heartache
isn't welcome here
Baby I promise
To stay loyal and honest,
My only wish is
to live here, with you
for the rest of our days
Look into my heart
To feel how much
I love being home with you,
So warm and secure
When the world rains
Know one thing for sure
Your man, will do anything
To protect you from storms

Dream: UNLoved Child

Sara & I were walking through the park. We overheard a woman cursing at her infant. They were sitting on a bench. The woman was ~~disgust~~ disgusted by this beautiful baby. The ~~child~~ infant had downs ~~s~~ syndrome. Despite the hate her mother was ~~given~~ giving her, she smiled and giggled. ~~We~~ We walked up to the woman and said

"If you wont love, we will."

I ~~grabbed~~ grabbed the baby and walked away. The mother didnt resist.

Kids Say The Darnedest Things

I worked for the YMCA
After school
And summer program,
During my tenure
I met many
Children who told stories
Too heavy for my heart to carry.
I heard words like:
"My dad hates me because
my mom is a stripper",
"My dad punched my grandma this
morning."
"My parents think I'm stupid",
"Mom thinks I'm too fat",
"Mom only keeps me
for the money she gets,"
A girl with autism said.
One little girl wrote
"I want to kill myself,
because I hate being black",
on a note.
One girl told me
her mother constantly shamed
her dark complexion.

Dreaming in a Perfect World

Some of the mothers
Would arrive
Drunk or half strung out
With lipstick
smeared on their lips,

I watched a child's face
Go from joy to fear
The moment her father appeared
Realizing the best part
of her day was over
Some children are orphans
In their own home
Because their parents
Are dead inside,
They wish to run away
but they can't,
Instead remain
Hopeless, homeless,
Under a roof,
they feel lonely
I see why
the sad bird still sings
it just wants people
to feel its pain
The same reason why
Kids say the darnedest things.

Love thy Child, Unconditionally.

The moment you stare into
Your child's eyes
And hold them in your arms
You're making a vow to
Protect them with all your might
And love them with every ounce
Your heart has to offer,
Regardless of what they
grow up to be

If they're queer
love them unconditionally

If they choose
a different religious path,
Love them unconditionally,

If they decide to pursue a
Dream that doesn't
Align with yours
Love them unconditionally,

Your child is not obligated
To live the life you
Vicariously try to live
Through them

Dreaming in a Perfect World

But you are obligated
Love their entire being
Even If they choose a life
Better suited
for their growth
and joy

If you lack the capacity
To love unconditionally,
Please don't have children

The world doesn't need
More unwanted
and half loved children

The Ghost

There was a ghost shadowing me. It followed me everywhere, but it's presence was haunting and calming. It watched my every mood. I was so cautious, this spirit was ~~perfect~~ protecting me.

Dreaming in a Perfect World

"Intuition is a superpower given to you
to help guide you through difficult
situations and identify shady people.
Never second guess it. Let it be your
light."

Dreaming in a Perfect World

"Trust your intuition when it warns you
about someone's character. It's right
100% of the time."

The Spirits

I pray the spirits
guide and protect me
from the darkness
whenever I feel lost.

I pray the angels
give a shoulder
to lean on
when my mind spirals
out of control.

I pray the spirits
Who are assigned to me
Block chaos
from coming into my life

I pray the angels
Will continue to
Fill my life with love
And good people

＾

The Healing Journey

The healing journey has no room for
fear, so be prepared to get your hands
dirty. Be prepared to feel lost when
you're traveling alone. Be prepared to
take a few detours because healing
isn't linear. Be prepared to get tested
by unforeseen obstacles. I hope you're
ready to embark on the road less
traveled; with patience and courage,
you will arrive at the destination
filled with blissful sunshine and
hopeful clouds.

Dream: A Miricle.

I went into ~~croffed~~ work and greeted the
residents one of them had a fresh haircut,
& I comprmented him. He laughed and
bragged, but he's typically non-verbal and
has autism. In this dream he was far
from apathetic as he cracked jokes and
stood from his wheelchair without
struggle. He had a midwest accent too.
As I stared In shock my coworkers
~~praese~~. proceeded like nothing was ~~strange~~
strange.

Dreaming in a Perfect World

"After all the pain
Beauty still resides inside you
It may take years of
digging to reach
but it will
be worth the work."

The Seed that Grew

When your life is on the brink of chaos
and everything you love is crumbling
before your raining eyes, remember
there's a silver lining in every dark
cloud, and miracles only happen when
you believe in magic. Continue to be
open and vulnerable; this period of
your life is shaping you into a
warrior. Think of the seed that
blossomed to life after the many storms
that rained on its soil. It found a way
to grow through the dark madness, so
will you.

Dreaming in a Perfect World

~~Bottom~~ Rih the camgirl

I was browsing through a popular
camming site and saw Rihanna as
the Featured Model, to my surprise & disbelief
It was her. She was dancing to her
songs getting tipped by the hundreds.
She was whining in lingerie, teasing and
laughing. I was mesmerized and
joyful while pleasing myself. A historic
night It was

Dreaming in a Perfect World

Sex Workers

Sexuality is natural
Like rainfall and sunshine
But we're forced to suppress
our urges and desires
To appeal to
man-made constructs like
religion and societal views,
Wasting our youth
Slaving for
a billion-dollar company
That doesn't
give a fuck about us
Is normalized
But we're shamed for
Using our bodies for profit,
The temple we own
is viewed As taboo when we
Show pride in our sensuality
Why does nudity
Make the prudes uncomfortable?
Why is making money off sex
Deemed as gross and shameful?
Sex is human nature
Fucking is why we are all alive
So when someone decides
to pursue sex work
Save your outdated arguments
on religion and morals,
keep your desk job And 9-5s,
Let the free spirits
Do what they please
With their bodies in peace

Free Spirit, Wild Heart

She's a free spirit
So they try to contain her

She's comfortable in her skin
So they try to make her feel
less beautiful

She owns her sexuality
So they try to take it away
By slut-shaming

She's in control
of her temple
So they try
to police her body
With outdated morals
and Man-made laws.

Why is the oppressor obsessed
With controlling women
Why do women have to fight
For the ownership of their
divine temple?

Why does the empowered woman
Offend the right-wingers
and religious buffs?

The ex

Sara & I were at a restaurant.
She recieved a text from her ex.
"Dont even respond," I said.
She insisted to, but in a way that would
piss him off. She wanted to exaggerate
her lifestyle to make him jealous.
We went back and forth. I went outside
for fresh air. When I went back
inside her phone was blowing up.
She told me, that she sent the message
I stared with pure shame. We argued
and stopped outside. She kissed
me and said sorry, then He pulled up.
She got in his car. I said goodbye
to her family. So much pain felt
In so little time.

Achilles Heel

When you find yourself
Too comfortable to move on
from the person
who uses your heart
as a battlefield
You'll be stuck running
In a hamster wheel
With no way out,
Despair becomes your new normal
And happiness becomes
An illusion your mind
Conjures to keep
The façade you call a smile
You grow so accustomed
to heartache
And fool your mind
to believe
True love is pain,
and everyday
will feel like
the same cycle of you
running in place
Comfort is growth's
Achilles heel.

What "Let's take a Break Really Mean"

Let's take a break to break-up
Let's prolong the inevitable
Reality of us
no longer being together
Let's get drunk off denial
and wake up with
a heartbreak hangover
let's fool ourselves
into believing
some time apart will
make us stronger
Let's try to convince our minds
That falling apart
Will only help us
come back together
Let's keep lying to each other
So we can find comfort
in our broken hearts.
Let's give each other time
to find ourselves
before finding someone else

"Let's take a break."
 Is a softer way of saying
"we're through,
 but I want you to leave,
before I do."

Shene Part I

We were at Shene Aiko's house,
looking through her bookshelf. My book
"God is a woman" was there I was
so excited to see it, I approached
her In the livingroom. She was sipping
tea with Jerry Seinfeld. I asked
her about my book, she said "I bought
it years ago, It was okay!"
She didn't realize it was written by
me.
Seinfeld followed with "who
names thier book God is a woman?"
to embaressed to say
I just walked away.

Artist to Artist

I know as an artist it's our dream to
be admired by the creatives we look up
to, but their opinion of their work
should not make or break your
confidence. So if they love your work,
be flattered but don't let it inflate
your ego, and if they don't enjoy or
acknowledge your art don't let it
deflate your confidence. Believe in
your work no matter what celebs may
think of it.

Dreaming in a Perfect World

The Celebrity Effect

When I was a no named
Author promoting my work
The locals didn't care,
Their energy was dull
When I told them about my work

Now when they see celebs like
Jhene Aiko, Alicia Keys,
and Rosario Dawson following me
The women who ignored me
Ask "Do you remember me?"
People who were
once silent
spectators pretend
to be proud of me

Even when my audience
was gradually growing they
didn't bat an eye
Until
Sophia Bush,
Snoh Allegra,
Vanessa Hudgens
Bella Thorne
Bagan to share my work

Dreaming in a Perfect World

Its sad,
How locals refuse
to support their own
artists until
the hype comes along

This isn't a brag
Or a petty shot at my locals

It's for my fellow artists
who struggle
with gaining support.

Don't focus on your locals,
And never give up.
Don't fall
into the trap of self-doubt

There's a whole world
Outside of your city
Ready to fall in love
with your art,
You just have to be present
And give them the chance
to appreciate you

Dreaming in a Perfect World

The End

Printed in Great Britain
by Amazon

62882965R00132